# Beginners' Programme *to* Piano & Synthesizer

*(Grade-1)*

*By*

Nitin Srivastava

*(Guitarmonk)*

UNICORN BOOKS

*Publisher*
**UNICORN BOOKS**
F-2/16, Ansari Road, Daryaganj, New Delhi-110002
☎ 011-23275434, 23262683, 23250704 • *Fax:* 011-23257790
*E-mail:* info@unicornbooks.in • *Website:* www.unicornbooks.in

**Branch : Mumbai**
23-25, Zaoba Wadi, Thakurdwar, Mumbai-400002
☎ 022-22010941, 022-22053387
*E-mail:* rapidex@bom5.vsnl.net.in



ISBN 978-81-7806-226-6
*(Piano-Keyboard Grade 1)*

**Edition:** 2017



***Printed at :*** Param Offsetters, Okhla, New Delhi-110020

# Preface

I have great pleasure to bring forth this book as part of my endeavour to give some sort of organisation and structure to the music education in India.

Going by my professional experience in the last two decades, I have realized that India badly needs an organized music teaching system. The non-existence of such a system is one of the factors that plagues music education in our country. Non-compulsory music education and lack of awareness are the other factors which add to its present state.

This is the first book of the four volume book series published under the same title. As there is a dearth of constructive content for study and reference on this subject, to a great extent, this book will serve the purpose. The well organized content and the exercises of this book are a first-class study material for the aspiring students of music to prepare for various examinations. Even a 5 year old learner can use this book and it will help him to achieve the desired goal in a short span of time.

It is a matter of great pride and pleasure to note that my other books on music are well received by students and readers alike across the globe. They are also introduced as text books in many schools. We reach out all the places and regions through these books and thus we would be able to serve you without our physical presence.

I thank readers, students and others for their support and patronage. Your suggestions and comments on the further improvement of this book will be thankfully acknowledged and the same will be incorporated in the next edition.

**Author**

# Overview

## THE OBJECTIVES

The primary objective of this book is to familiarise the learners with terminologies, exercises and repertoires along with the audios of the compositions. This would help the learners to get a clear perspective on various aspects of the subject.

## WHOM IS THIS BOOK FOR?

The book is for complete beginners who know nothing about the instrument, the students who prepare for examinations and the teachers who train the students.

## THE SPECIAL FEATURES

- It is customized into levels and can be covered very easily in 12-24 sessions maximum based on time involvement.
- It is an ideal book for teachers who help their student in constructive sessions and productive outcome.
- The book is a step-by-step guide which takes a student from one level to the next. It also inspires success at every grade via achievements which motivates students to get curious and interested in further learning.
- This book contains an audio-CD that instructs on speed and movement of tune: and it is a good reference for the learners who find difficulties in staff reading.
- It contains the basics of staff notations which is very useful information for any music beginner.
- It is a compilation of very significant compositions, rated at a global standard, essential for any music student.

- It offers finger movements which are the most important part for a quality and right learning and support to both teacher and student.
- It offers exercise, pop music repertoire, music theory and Practice Compositions

## HOW WILL THIS BOOK HELP YOU?

- It can help you in going about a step-by-step and systematic learning
- A quality and constructive repertoire of songs for your personal performance.
- It instructs you on finger patterns, so as to help both teacher and student with accurate fingering.
- You can expect a basic performance from yourself and can render a medley of tunes on any platform after practicing the given tunes.
- It can assist you, to a great extent, for a performance preparation and content and, thus, it can bring out a musician in you.

# Content

**Western Pop Songs Repertoire**

# EXERCISES

## TECHNICAL DEVELOPMENT

(An essential practice for every music student)

# Exercise - 1

(Right Hand Finger Exercises)

Finger Patterns on White Keys

**Moderate** ♩ **= 120**

**PATTERN - 1**

**PATTERN - 2**

**PATTERN - 3**

# Exercise - 2

(Right Hand Finger Exercises)

Finger Patterns on White Keys

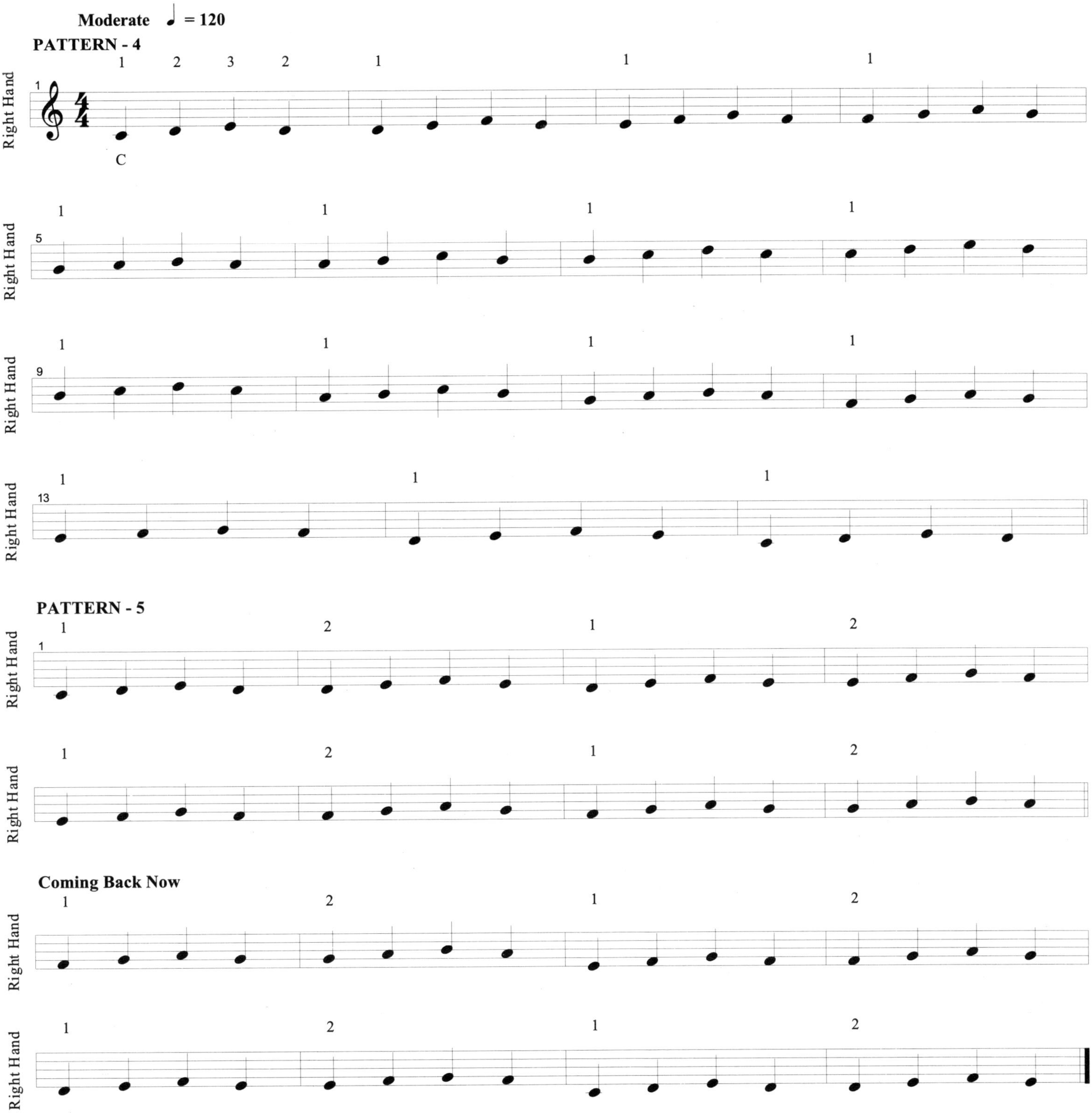

# Exercise - 3

(Right Hand Finger Exercises)

Finger Patterns on White Keys

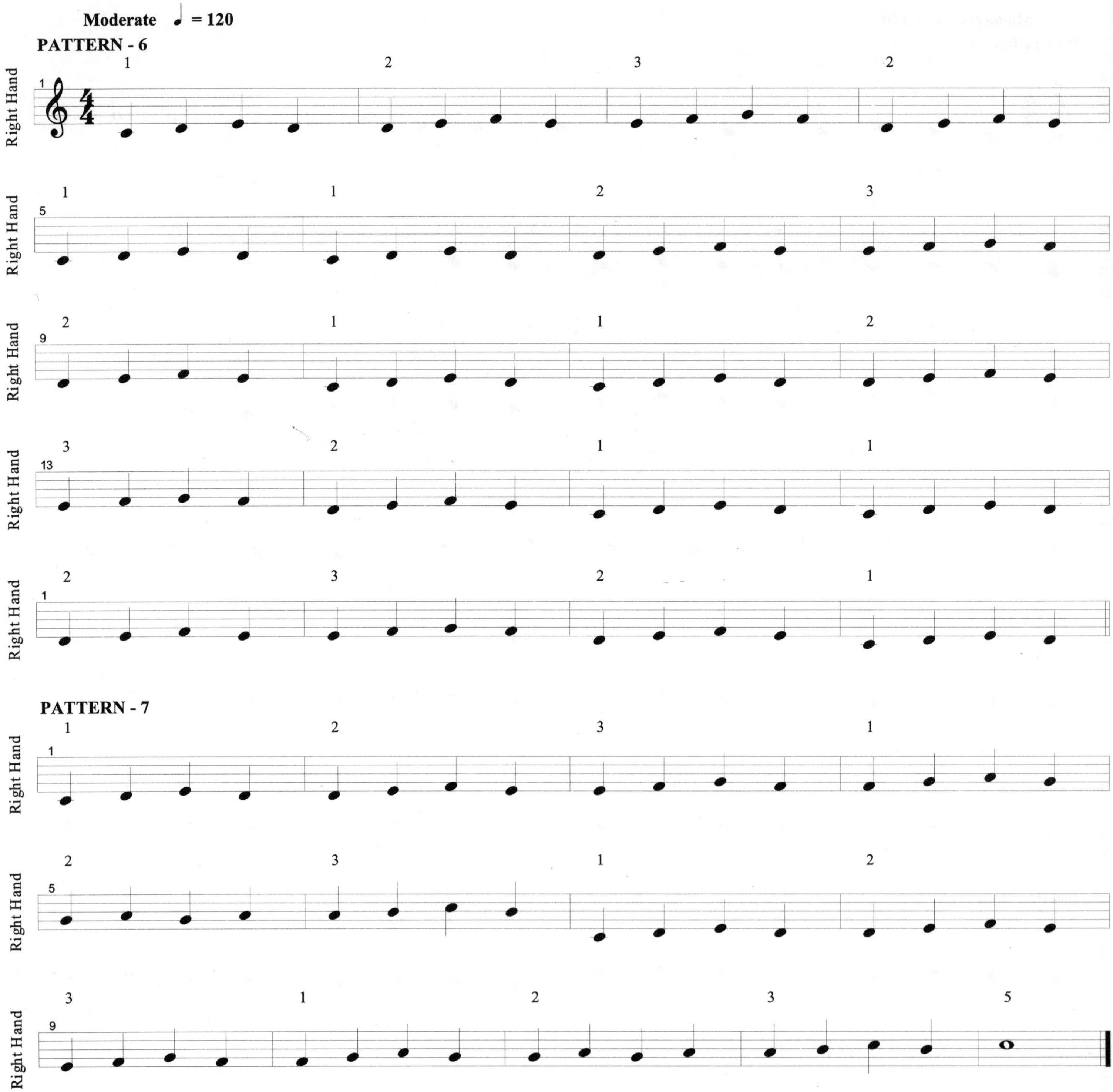

# Exercise - 4

(Right Hand Finger Exercises)

Finger Patterns on White Keys

**Moderate** ♩ = 120

**PATTERN - 8**

**PATTERN - 9**

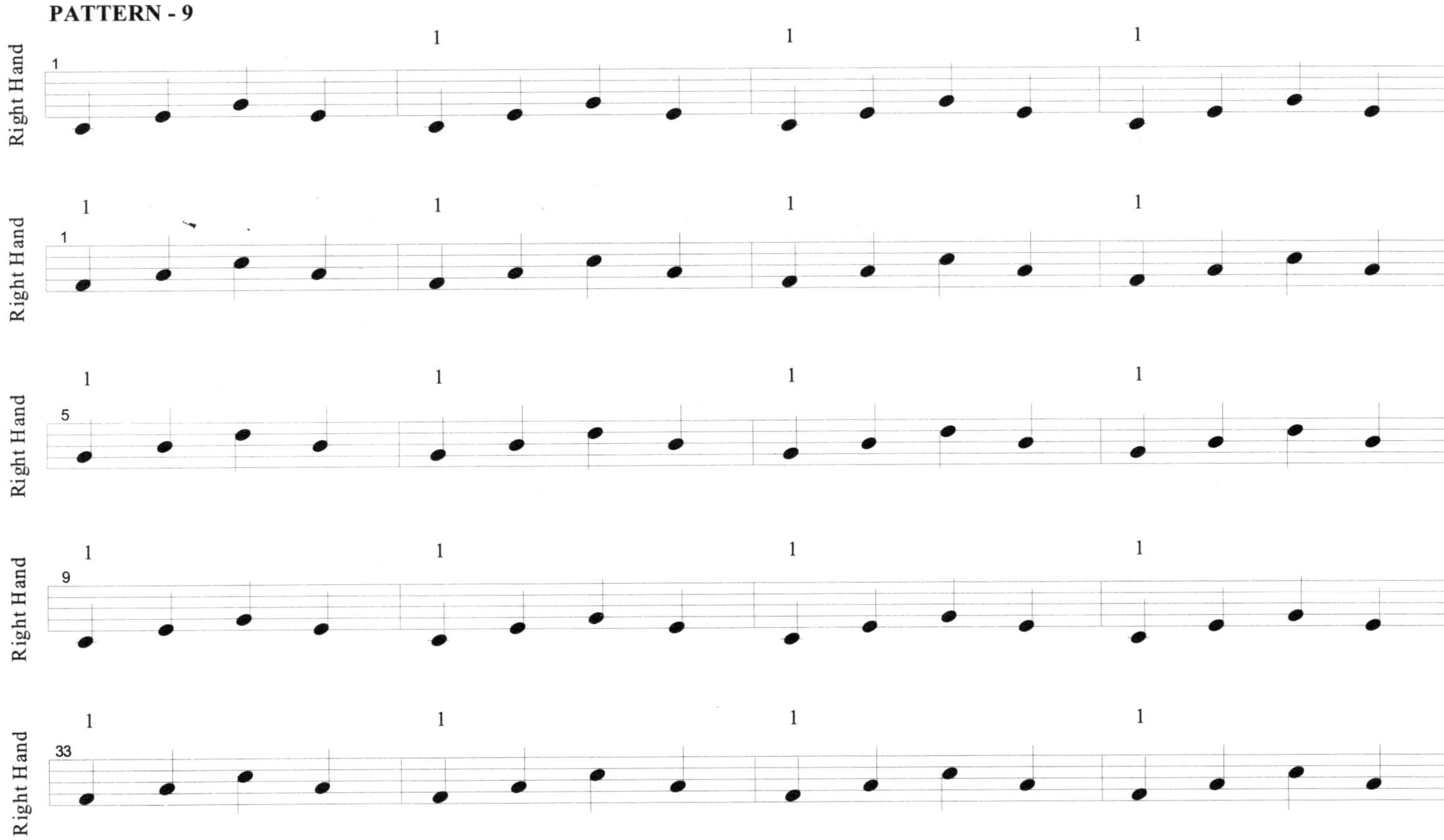

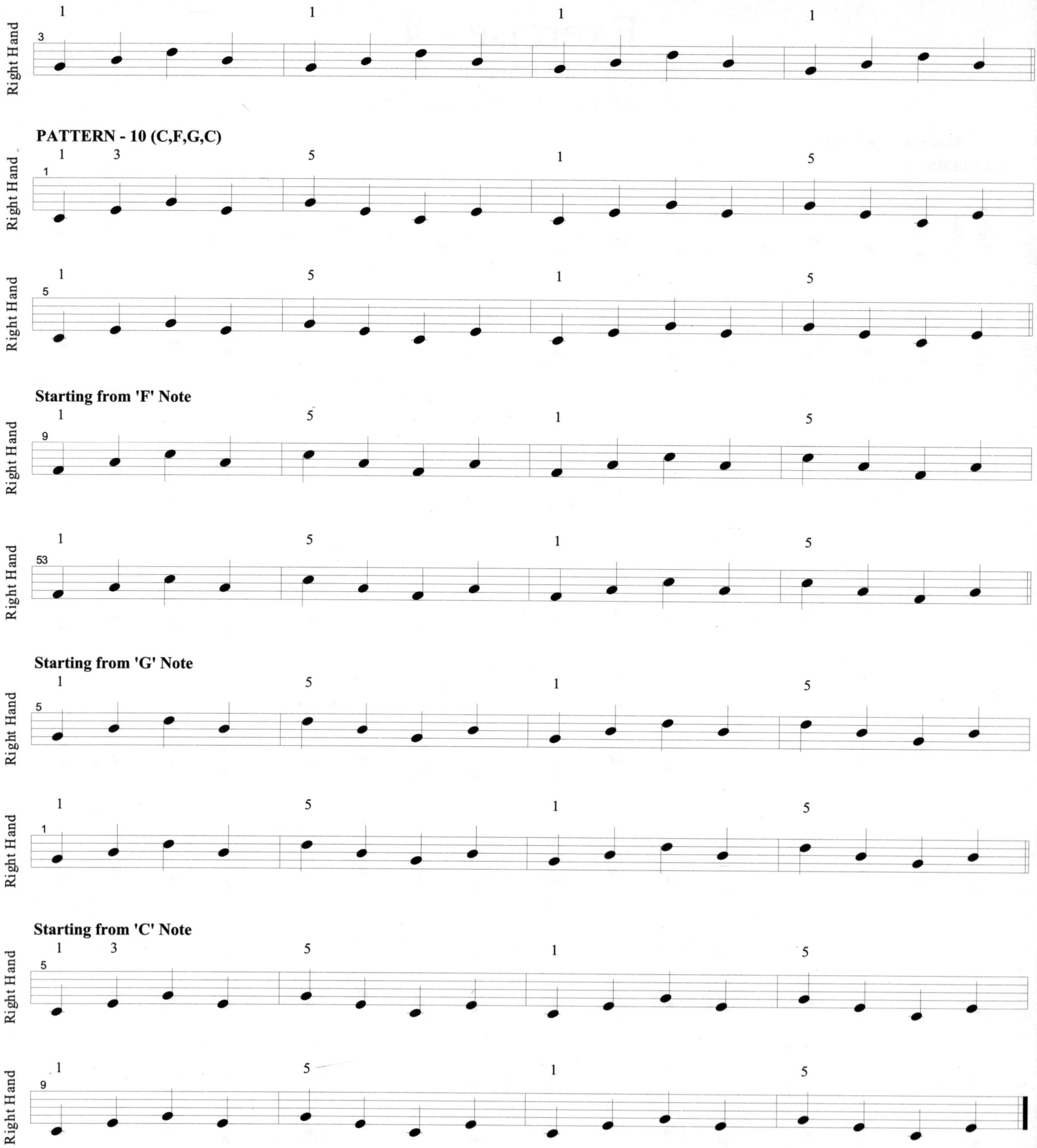
Right Hand
PATTERN - 10 (C,F,G,C)
Starting from 'F' Note
Starting from 'G' Note
Starting from 'C' Note

# Exercise - 5

## (Right Hand Finger Exercises)

## Finger Patterns on White Keys

**Moderate** ♩ = 120

**PATTERN - 11**

**PATTERN - 12**

**PATTERN - 13 (Combining Patterns 11 & 12)**

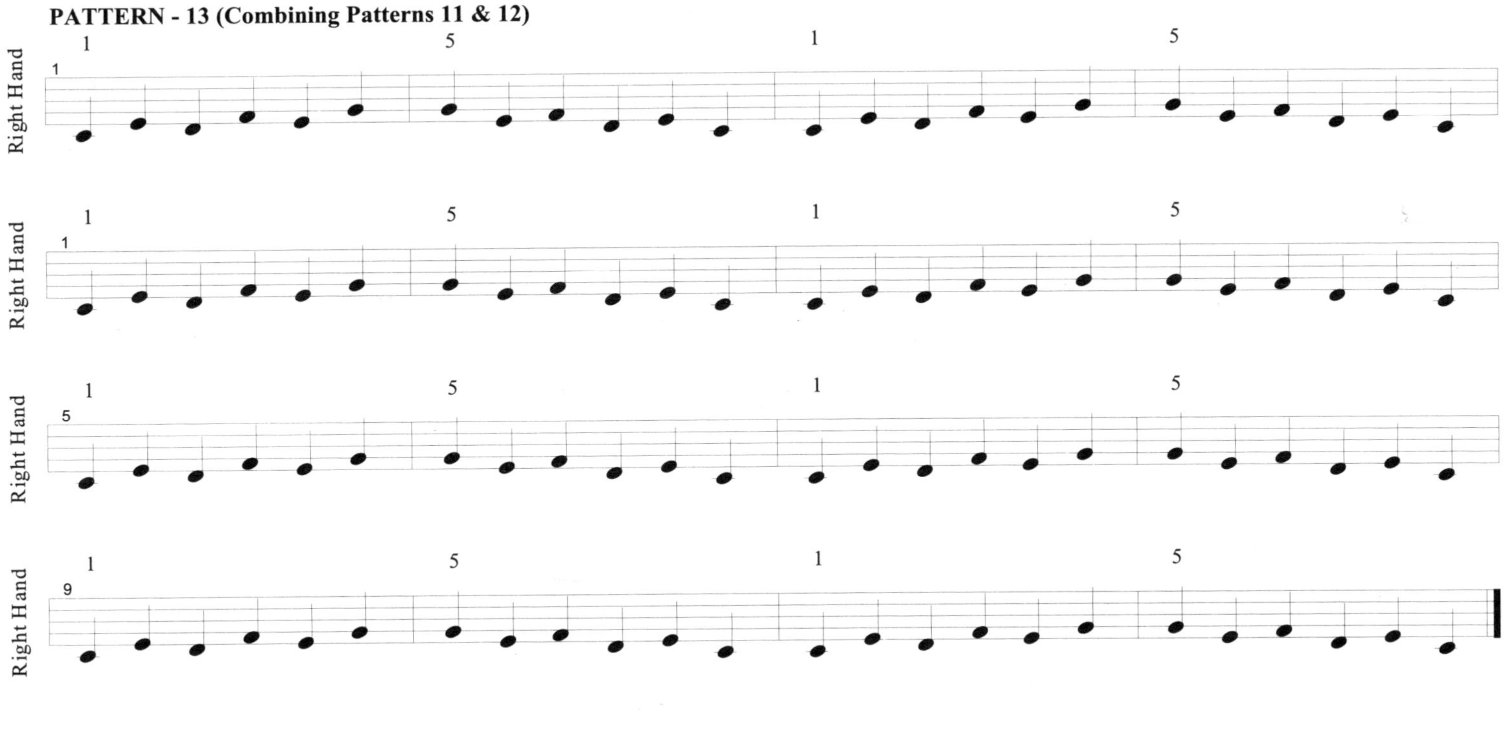

## What is a Scale?

**Scale:** The word Scale derived from the Latin word 'Scale' meaning ladder. So just like a ladder, Scale is a series of steps of notes that can be taken in ascending and descending order.

**Major Scale:** A major scale consists of 7 notes selected out of the set of 12 notes. The major scale has a fixed standard formula that defines the distance between each note at every step or degree. The formula for any major scale is:

**W-W-H-W-W-W-H**

Where 'W' is the **Whole Note/ 1 step** & 'H' is **Half Note/half Step**

| | **1** | **2** | **3** | **4** | **5** | **6** | **7** | **8** |
|---|---|---|---|---|---|---|---|---|
| 'C' Major Scale: | C | D | E | F | G | A | B | C |
| 'G' Major Scale: | G | A | B | C | D | E | **F#** | G |
| 'F' Major Scale: | F | G | A | **Bb** | C | D | E | F |

Here, we will be covering three important scale practices essential for every beginner. The beginner should know that what note is getting changed in a scale and which finger is to be used. The beginner student should also practice each scale in ascending and descending order a number of times to build finger dexterity.

The following diagrams will help you to see the change of finger in a particular scale.

## C Major Scale Notes & Fingering

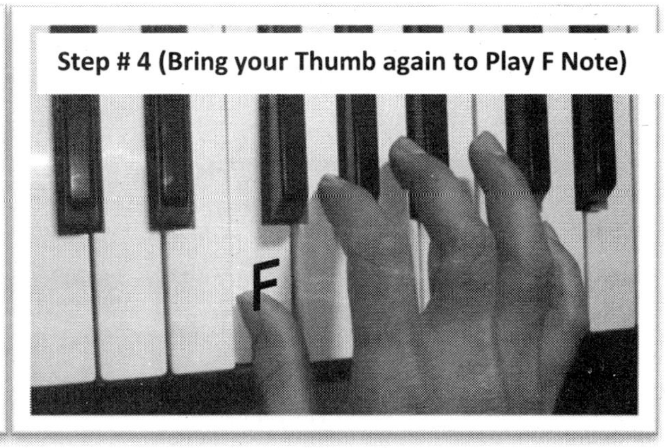

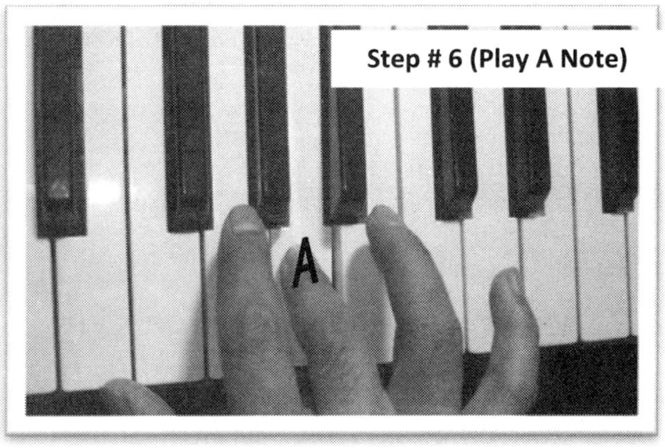

You have learnt

1. Finger Position of C Major Scale
2. Step 1 to Step 8 of playing all 8 notes
3. Relative finger to be used for particular note

## F MAJOR AND G MAJOR SCALE

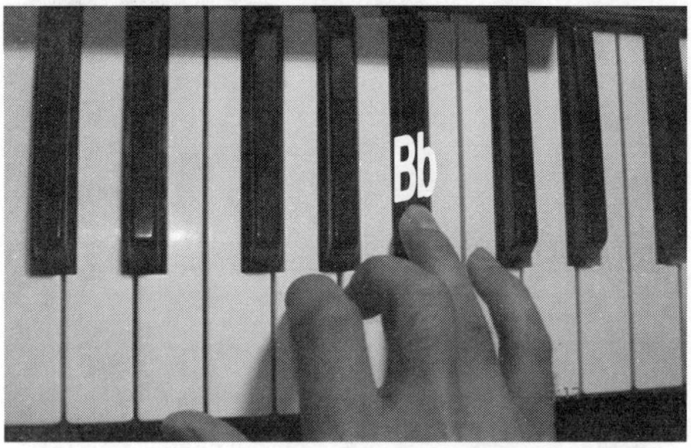


**F Major Scale** will have one key change i.e. Bb instead of B Note and will be played by 4th Finger (Ring Finger)

**G Major Scale** will have one key change i.e. F# instead of F Note (if we compare it to C Major Scale) and will be played instead of F note and will be played with 4th finger (Ring Finger)

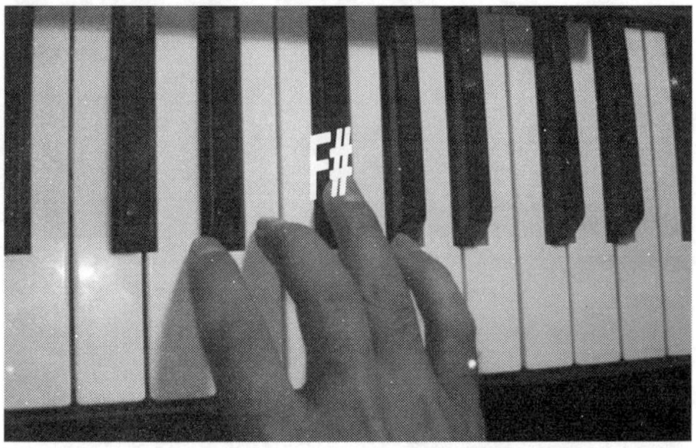


### What is a Chord and what are its basic types?

When you take more than 2 notes simultaneously it becomes a chord. There are two basic types of chords

- Major(Primary)
- Minor(Secondary)

Each scale contains 3 major or 3 minor chords. The three most important positions that a beginner needs to know is covered here.

# BASIC CHORD POSITIONS IN WHITE KEYS

## MAJOR CHORDS (PRIMARY CHORDS)

### C Major Chord

Combination of 3 notes:

C + E + G

### F Major Chord

Combination of 3 notes:

F + A + C

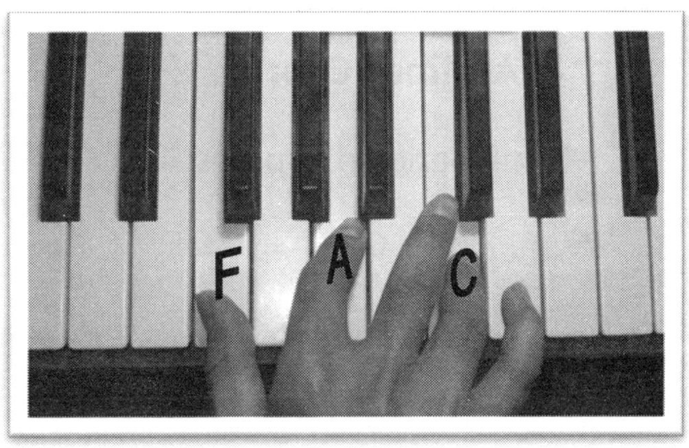


### G Major Chord

Combination of 3 notes:

G + B + D

## BASIC CHORD POSITIONS IN WHITE KEYS

## MINOR CHORS (SECONDARY CHORDS)

### E Minor Chord

Combination of 3 notes:

E + G + B

### A Minor Chord

Combination of 3 notes:

A + C + E

### D Minor Chord

Combination of 3 notes:

D + F + A

# COMPOSITIONS

(A collection of special practice repertoire...)

# Ainsi Font, Font, Font

Beginners' Keyboard Certification

Pianomonk

# Clementine

Beginner's Keyboard Certification

Pianomonk

**Moderate** ♩ = 120

# I Have a Little Dreidle

Beginner's Keyboard Certification

Pianomonk

# London Bridge

Beginner's Keyboard Certification

Pianomonk

# Morning Song

Beginners' Keyboard Certification

Pianomonk

# O Christmas Tree

Beginners' Keyboard Certification

Pianomonk

**Moderate** ♩ = 80

# Ode to Joy

Beginner's Keyboard Certification

Pianomonk

# Old MacDonald Had a Farm

Beginner's Keyboard Certification

Pianomonk

# This Old

Beginner's Keyboard Certification

Pianomonk

# Twinkle, Twinkle Little Star

Beginner's Keyboard Certification

Pianomonk

# Ainsi Font, Font, Font

Beginner's Keyboard Certification

Pianomonk

# Ode to Joy

Beginner's Keyboard Certification

Pianomonk

# Western Pop Songs

# MUSIC CHORDS AND LYRICS

**(A beautiful repertoire for all music lovers and students...)**

# WESTERN SONGS

1. Everything I do
2. Words
3. My heart will go on
4. Back to you
5. Right here waiting
6. Unbreakable
7. Truly Madly Deeply
8. I Need you

# EVERYTHING I DO

**Artist:** Bryan Adams
**Album:** Waking up the Neighbour
**Scale:** Eb Major

**Eb** **Bb**
Look into my eyes, you will see,
**Ab** **Bb**
What you mean to me,
**Eb** **Bb**
Search your heart; search your soul,
**Ab** **Bb**
And when you find me there you'll search no more..
**Fm** **Bb**
Don't tell me it's not worth trying for,
**Ab** **Bb**
You can't tell me; it's not worth dying for,
**Eb** **Bb** **Eb**
You know it's true... Everything I do, I do it for you,

**Eb** **Bb**
Look into my heart, you will find,
**Ab** **Bb**
There's nothing there to hide
**Eb** **Bb**
Take me, as I am, take my life.
**Ab** **Bb**
I would give it, I would sacrifice,

**Fm** **Bb**
Don't tell me it's not worth fighting for
**Ab** **Bb**
I can't help it; it's nothing I want more.
**Eb** **Bb** **Eb**
You know it's true... Everything I do, I do it for you.

**Fm** **Bb**
Oh! Yeah! You can't tell me it's not worth trying for,
**Fm** **Bb**
I can't help it; it's nothing I want more,
**Eb** **Bb**
Yeah! I'll fight for you, I die for you,
**Ab**
Walk the wire for you
**Abm**
Yeah! I die for you
**Eb** **Bb** **Eb**
You know it's true... Everything I do, I do it for you.

There's no love;
like your love,

And no other could,
give me more love,

There's no way,
unless you are there,

All the time,
all the way...

You know it's true,
Everything I Do...

# WORDS

2

**Artist:** Boyzone
**Album:** A Different Beat
**Scale:** G Major

```
G
Smile an everlasting smile,
                         A
A smile can bring you near to me,
        D
Don't ever let me find you gone,
                            C       G
Cause that would bring a tear to me
```

```
    Bb
This world has lost its glory,
                             F
Let's start a brand new story now, my love
    Bb
You think that I don't even mean,
               D
A single word I say,
   G                        D
It's only words and words are all I have,
                    G
To take your heart away,
```

```
G
Talk in everlasting words,
                    A
and dedicate them all to me
    D
and I will give you all my life
                         C      G
I'm there if you should call on me
```

Smile an everlasting Smile,

A smile can bring you,

Near to Me,

Don't ever let me find that

You are gone,

Cause that would bring a,

Tear to me...

# MY HEART WILL GO ON



**Artist:** Celine Dion
**Album:** Titanic
**Scale:** E Major

**E A E B**
Every night in my dreams I see you I feel you,
**E A B**
That is how I know you go on.
**E A E B**
Far across the distance and spaces between us,
**E A B**
You have come to show you go on.

**E B A B**
Near far wherever you are,
**E A B**
I believe that the heart does go on
**E B A B**
Once more you open the door,
**E B**
And you're here in my heart,
**A B E**
And my heart will go on and on

**E A E B**
Love can touch us one time and last for a life time
**E A B**
And never let go till we're gone
**E A E B**
Love was when I loved you, one true time I hold to,
**E A B**
In my life we'll always go on

**Fm Eb Db Eb**
Your here, there's nothing I fear
**Fm Eb Db Cm Bbm**
And I know that my heart will go on
**Fm Eb Db Eb**
We'll stay forever this way
**Fm Eb**
You are safe in my heart
**Db Eb Fm Eb Db**
And my heart will go on and on

Every night in my dreams,
I see you, I feel you,

That I how I know you,
go on,
Far across the distance,
And spaces between us,

You have come to show,
you go on,

# BACK TO YOU

4

**Artist:** Bryan Adams
**Album:** Unplugged
**Scale:** C Major

**C Am**
I've been down, I've been beat,
**F Gsus4**
I've been so tired that I couldn't speak,
**C Am**
I've been so lost that I could not see,
**F Gsus4**
I wanted things that were out of reach,
**C Am**
Then I found you, and you helped me through,
**F Gsus4**
And you showed me what to do,
**F E**
That's why, I'm coming back to you,
**Am F Gsus4 G**
Like a star that guides a ship, across the ocean,
**Am F Gsus4 G**
That's how your love can take me home, back to you,
**Em Am Em Am**
And if I wish upon that star, that someday I'll be where you are
**F Gsus4 G**
I know that day is coming soon; yeah I'm coming back to you,

**C Am F Gsus4**

**Am F Gsus4 G**

**G Am F Gsus4**
I'm coming back to you
**G Am F Gsus4**
I'm coming back to you
**G Am F Gsus4**
I'm coming back to you
**G Am F Gsus4**
I'm coming back to you
**G Am F Gsus4**
That day is coming soon
**G Am F Gsus4**
I'm coming back to you
**G Am F C/G**

I've been down,

I've been beat,

I've been so tired that I

Couldn't see,

I wanted things that were,

Out of reach...,

# RIGHT HERE WAITING

5

**Artist:** Richard Marx
**Album:** Repeat Offender
**Scale:** C Major

**C F Dm**
Oceans apart day after day
**G7 C**
And I slowly go insane
**C F Dm**
I hear your voice on the line
**G/B Am**
But it doesn't stop the pain
**F**
If I see you next to never
**Am Dm G7**
How can we say forever?

**C F Dm**
I took for granted, all this times,
**G7 C**
That I thought would last somehow
**C F Dm**
I hear the laughter, I taste the tears
**G/B Am**
But I can't get you near you now
**F**
Oh, can't you see it baby
**Am Dm G7**
You've got me goin' crazy...

**C G E7 Am**
Wherever you go, whatever you do,
**F G7 C**
I will be right here waiting for you.
**C G E7 Am**
Whatever it takes or how my heart breaks,
**F G7 Am**
I will be right here waiting for you.

I wonder how we can survive this romance,

But in the end if I'm with you,

I will take the chance,

Wherever you go, whatever you do,

I will be right here waiting for you...,

# UNBREAKABLE

6

**Artist:** Westlife
**Album:** Unbreakable
**Scale:** G Major

```
G                                  Em
Took my hand, touch my heart,
            C                 D
Held me close, you were always there,
          G          Em
By my side, night and day,
               C       D
Through it all, baby come what may,
         Em                      G
Swept away on a wave of emotion,
            C                          G
We were caught in the eyes of the storm,
         Em                        G                           Am
And whenever you smile I can hardly believe that you're mine
                        D
Believe that you're mine...
```

Share the Laughter, share the tears,
We both know, we will go on from here,
Cause together, we are strong,
In my arms that's where you belong,
I have been touched by the hands of an angel,
I have been blessed by the power of the love
And whenever you smile I can hardly believe that you're mine
Believe that you're mine...

This love is unbreakable,

It's unmistakable and each time I look in your eyes, I know why...,

This love is untouchable,

A feeling my heart just can't deny and each time I look in your eyes oh baby,

I know why...,

This love is Unbreakable...

```
                 G                      Em
This love is unbreakable, it's unmistakable
              C                              D
Each time I look in your eyes, I know why
                 G                            Em
This love is untouchable, a feeling my heart just can't deny
                 C                        G             D
Each time I look in your eyes, oh baby, I know why
                  Em
This love is unbreakable
```

# TRULY MADLY DEEPLY

7

**Artist:** Darren Hayes
**Album:** Savage Garden
**Scale:** C Major

**C** **G**
I'll be your dream, I'll be your wish I'll be your fantasy.
**F** **G**
I'll be your hope; I'll be your love be everything that you need.
**C** **G**
I love you more with every breath truly madly deeply do..
**F** **G**
I will be strong I will be faithful 'coz I'm counting on
**C** **G**
A new beginning, a reason for living
**F** **G**
A deeper meaning

**C** **G**
And when the stars are shining brightly in the velvet sky,
**F** **G**
I'll make a wish send it to heaven then make you want to cry,
**C** **G**
The tears of joy for all the pleasure and the certainty,
**F** **G**
That we're surrounded by the comfort and protection of the
**C** **G**
Highest power, in lonely hours
**F** **G**
The tears devour you.

I'll be your dream,

I'll be your wish,

I'll be yourfantasy,

I'll be your hope,

I'll be your love,

Be everything that you need,

**C** **G**
I want to stand with you on a mountain.
**F** **G**
I want to bathe with you in the sea.
**C** **G**
I want to lay like this forever.
**F** **G**
Until the sky falls down on me

# I NEED YOU

8

**Artist:** Mark Anthony
**Album:** Mended
**Scale:** C Major

```
C
From the day that I met you girl
                G
I knew that your love would be
          F                     C
Everything that I ever wanted in my life
                           C
From the moment you spoke my name
           G
i knew everything had changed
          F                          C
Because of you I felt my life would be complete
```

Nothing matters but you my love and

Only God above could be the one to know

Exactly how I feel

I could die in your arms right now,

Knowing that you somehow

Would take my soul and keep it deep inside your heart

Oh baby

I need you

For the rest of my girl

I need you

Say that you'll be my life,

I love you, wont you marry me, marry me.

I need you

I need you...

Oh baby

```
F G  C
I need you
C
To make everything right girl
F G  C
I love you
C
And I'll never deny that
F G  C
I need you
```